Summer's Vacation

By Lynn Plourde

Illustrated by Greg Couch

Simon & Schuster Books for Young Readers

NEW YORK LONDON TORONTO SYDNEY SINGAPORE

A Note from the Artist

I work on museum board; it's like a very thick, smooth watercolor paper. I put down many washes of liquid acrylic paint until I get the mood I'm looking for. Then I add details for the faces, clothes, etc. with colored pencils. If the colors aren't bright enough after that, I go back with a small brush and more acrylic to add the finishing touches.

SIMON & SCHUSTER BOOKS FOR YOUNG READERS

An imprint of Simon & Schuster Children's Publishing Division

1230 Avenue of the Americas, New York, New York 10020

Text copyright © 2003 by Lynn Plourde

Illustrations copyright © 2003 by Greg Couch

All rights reserved, including the right of reproduction in whole or in part in any form.

SIMON & SCHUSTER BOOKS FOR YOUNG READERS is a trademark of Simon & Schuster.

Book design by Mark Siegel

The text of this book is set in 22-point Lomba Medium.

Manufactured in China

10 9 8 7 6 5 4 3 2 1

Library of Congress Cataloging-in-Publication Data

Plourde, Lynn.

Summer's vacation / by Lynn Plourde; illustrated by Greg Couch.

p. cm.

Summary: Despite reminders from Father Time and Mother Earth, Summer neglects her chores while she is on vacation.

ISBN 0-689-84223-6

[1. Summer—Fiction. 2. Vacations—Fiction. 3. Behavior—Fiction. 4. Stories in rhyme.]

I. Couch, Greg, ill. II. Title.

PZ8.3.P5586922 Su 2003

[E]—dc21

2001032039

For Greg—Thank you for sharing this journey
through the seasons and for illustrations more magnificent
than I ever could have imagined.
—L. P.

To Paul, Rebecca, and Stephanie when it was new;
Mark, Jessica, Steve, and Brenda now that I'm through.
Thanks for all your patience and support.
And that goes double for Robin.
—G. C.

Summer cartwheels and shouts,
"Hip-hip-hooray!
Vacation is here.
Let's play, play, play."

She tugs Mother Earth's dress,
grabs Father Time's hand.
"Let's romp and frolic
all across the land."

Mother and Father grin and agree,
"Yes, vacations are fun.
But don't forget—
your chores must be done."

Summer promises,
"I'll do them soon.
But first, let's swim
all afternoon."

A race to the beach.
A dive with a splash.
Belly flops, cannonballs—
                    Thrashity-thrash.

Shape a sand castle
quick as a flash.
Till the waves swallow it—
                    Crashity-crash.

Mother Earth shakes her finger.
"Don't be too carefree.
Your chores are still waiting.
Now zippety-zee."

Summer promises,
"I'll do them in a while.
But first, let's hike.
Just for a mile."

Tramp on the trails
where the wildflowers sway.
Gobble up some berries.
Hide-and-seek in the hay.

Tiptoe in the forest
where it's cool and damp.
Now it's getting dark.
Time to set up camp.

Sing with the owls,
"Hoot-hoot-hoot!"
Hide from the skunks.
Scoot-scoot-scoot!

Under a blanket of clouds,
Summer gives a big yawn,
then snuggles and snoozes
until it is dawn.

She wakes her parents
with a "cock-a-doodle-doo."
"I'm ready to play.
How about you?"

Father Time stomps his foot.
"My daughter of play,
don't dilly-dally-dawdle.
Do your chores right away."

EXTENSION

Summer promises,
"I'll do them in a flash.
But first, let's try
a waterfall splash."

Mother and Father
exchange a glance
that says, "She gets
just one more chance."

The water gurgles and gushes—
making a spray,
as Summer plunges
and leapy frogs play.

Next, climb a mountain.
Grip and grapple tight.
Pull up to the peak.
What an awesome sight!

Gawk and gaze
at the view below.
"Look—something's wrong!"
She gasped, "Oh no!"

Summer shouts,
"What's that brown?
Covering the Earth
all around?"

"Mother, Father,
what is wrong?"
Their simple answer,
"You played too long."

Summer bursts into tears.
"I didn't mean to.
I'm so sorry.
Now what should I do?"

Mother Earth gives a hug.
Father Time dries a tear.
"You'll find a way,
our daughter so dear."

Summer promises,
"Yes, I'll make it right.
I'll work and work
with all my might."

And so Summer lugs
her sprinkling can,
day after day,
as fast as she can.

And slowly, so slowly—
there's a greenish glow.
The animals stir.
The rivers flow.

Mother Earth says proudly,
"You did great."
Father Time adds,
"Now take a break."

But Summer sighs.
"Not just yet.
One more thing,
so that I won't fret."

She pops open her paints
and splashes the sky
with a welcoming rainbow,
as she says good-bye.

"Oh, Autumn, my sister,
I wish I could stay,
so you and I
could play, play, play.

"But, here, use my paints
to splatter and spread
the whole world over—
yellow, orange, and red."